Maria Thun

THE BIODYNAMIC YEAR

Increasing yield, quality and flavour

100 helpful tips for the gardener or smallholder

TEMPLE LODGE

Maria Thun

THE BIODYNAMIC YEAR

Increasing yield, quality and flavour

100 helpful tips for the gardener or smallholder

Compiled and edited
by Angelika Throll-Keller

Translated by Matthew Barton

Temple Lodge Publishing
Hillside House, The Square
Forest Row, RH18 5ES

www.templelodge.com

First English edition, Temple Lodge 2007
Reprinted in paperback 2010

Originally published in German under the title
Mein Jahr im Garten by Franckh-Kosmos Verlags-GmbH & Co., Stuttgart

© Franckh-Kosmos Verlags-GmbH & Co. 2004

This translation © Temple Lodge Publishing 2007

With 129 colour photos by Heiko Bellmann; Gartenschatz; Häberli Obst and Beerenzentrum AG; Roland Krieg; Wolfgang Redeleit; Hans Reinhard; Ralf Roppelt; Jutta Schneider; Jürgen Stork and Maria Thun; and 31 colour drawings by Ruth Fritzsche

The author asserts her moral right to be identified as the authors of this work

A catalogue record for this book is available from the British Library

ISBN 978 1 906999 14 8

Cover by Andrew Morgan Design
Typeset by DP Photosetting, Neath, West Glamorgan
Printed and bound in Malta by Gutenberg Press Ltd.

Mixed Sources
Product group from well-managed forests, and other controlled sources
www.fsc.org Cert no. TT-CoC-002424
© 1996 Forest Stewardship Council

The paper used for this book is FSC-certified and totally chlorine-free. FSC (the Forest Stewardship Council) is an international network to promote responsible management of the world's forests.

CONTENTS

CONTENTS

CONTENTS

CONTENTS

PREFACE

As a child growing up on a farm I was allowed to help in the garden from an early age. I was glad whenever I could weed in my grandmother's wonderful flower beds. She had great pots of thyme, lavender, rosemary and garden myrrh (sweet cicely). In the winter she would bring these herbs into the house and put them in the hallway to protect them from frost, so that they filled the whole farmhouse with an indescribable scent.

My interest in cultivating salad and vegetables came later, when I started growing them for the whole family. But already as a ten-year-old I was transported by the different smells of salad herbs and the plants harvested daily for herb teas. Still today, whenever I pick hyssop, fennel and dill, childhood memories from those times rise up in me.

If my mother had been picking berries she let us smell them with closed eyes to see if we could tell which was which. We did the same thing with meadow flowers and medicinal herbs. Later, when I walked through the trees at night, I found that the leaves of different species of tree gave out quite specific perfumes. If you first walked beneath a heartily aromatic oak and then passed a thuja (arborvitae) hedge, its scent was a powerfully sobering experience. If you stroked a wormwood branch that was accidentally poking through a hedge, the bitter-sweet smell stayed with you for a long time afterwards.

Later on, when I came to read Rudolf Steiner's *Agriculture Course,* in which he says that farmers should become 'olfactorily clairsentient', this made a great deal of sense to me: you can discern good and bad qualities from plants' scent, aroma or bad smell.

I believe it is very important to help our children gain a closer connection to the plant world in this way, and then gardens can become a valuable source of strength for us. They can offer a small world of life and vitality, a sphere of creativity in which the gardener can also, occasionally, realize his childhood dreams.

Maria Thun

HOW WE NURTURE PLANTS

THE PLANT GROUPS

In our method of cultivation the influence of the moon, planets and stars on plant growth plays a central role. The forces and impulses emanating from the twelve signs of the zodiac (the Ram, Bull, etc. through to the Fishes)* exert a positive effect on the growth of plants.

We divide plants into four groups: leaf plants, root plants, blossom plants and fruit plants. Each group responds particularly to three zodiac regions.

1. Root plants: Bull, Virgin and Goat
2. Leaf plants: Fishes, Crab and Scorpion
3. Blossom plants: Waterman, Twins and Scales
4. Fruit plants: Ram, Lion and Archer

Whenever the moon passes in front of a star sign and we are preparing the soil for sowing or hoeing the beds, growth of the corresponding type of plant is specifically stimulated.

Which plants belong in which group? To put it simply: whichever part of the plant is used after harvest determines the group it belongs to. A lettuce belongs to the leaf plants, a rose to the blossom plants. There are just a few exceptions to this rule. See the following list and the easy-reference table on pages 102–5.

---

* The English rather than the Latin names of the zodiac constellations are given to distinguish them from the signs used in astrology, which are based on somewhat different calculations due to the 'precession of the equinoxes'. The planetary influences are, in this sense, astronomical rather than astrological.

We sowed radishes during ten different constellations. The best harvest came from those sown when the moon was in the Virgin or Goat. The worst results came from sowing at the Mercury nodes. We found that sowing radishes when the moon was in perigee (closest to the earth) made them split and burst open

Root plants

Almost all plants whose roots we use belong to this group: potatoes, onions, garlic, carrots, parsnips, turnips, radishes, beetroot, black salsify, celeriac, swedes, Hamburg parsley.

Leaf plants

These include almost all plants whose leaves we use: chicory, endive, lamb's lettuce, fennel leaf, most types of cabbage (including kohlrabi and cauliflower), lettuce, Swiss chard, grass, asparagus, spinach and all leaf herbs (chives, dill, thyme and others).

Blossom plants

In this group belong almost all the plants which we cultivate for their blossoms

Cauliflower sown at a Mars-Jupiter opposition always grow very big, and have a very good aroma

and which we want to flower for a long period: flowering bulbs, medicinal herb flowers, summer bedding plants, flowering shrubs and bushes, and also broccoli and the flowering plants that are used to make compost preparations for bio-dynamic compost.

Fruit plants

This group includes all the plants whose fruits we use: beans, peas, grains, cucumbers, pumpkins, lentils, sweet-corn, pepper, rice, soya, tomatoes and courgettes, and also all tree and bush fruits, and strawberries.

AFFINITIES

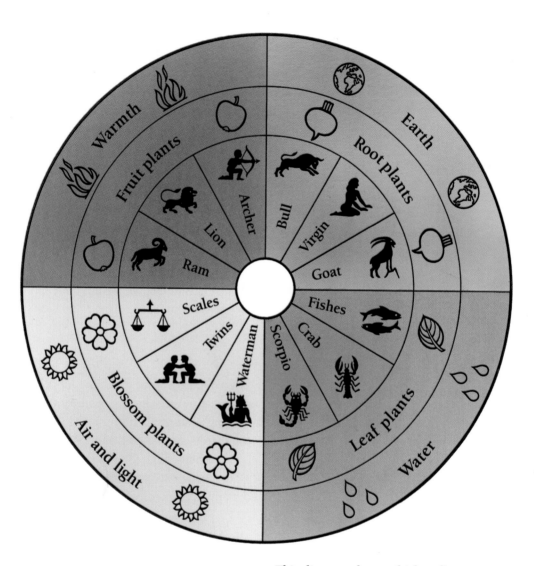

This diagram shows which zodiac constellations, plant groups and elements belong together

6

As already mentioned, we also divide the twelve zodiac signs into four groups. Each group, consisting of three star signs, belongs to one of the plant categories listed above. At the same time one element is assigned to each group.

The region of the Lion has a particularly positive effect on seed formation, highlighted in this table

Star sign	Plant group	Element
Fishes	Leaf	Water
Ram	Fruit	Warmth
Bull	Root	Earth
Twins	Blossom	Air/light
Crab	Leaf	Water
Lion	Fruit/seed	Warmth
Virgin	Root	Earth
Scales	Blossom	Air/light
Scorpion	Leaf	Water
Archer	Fruit	Warmth
Goat	Root	Earth
Waterman	Blossom	Air/light

My grandson and I in our own lab

7

ASCENDING AND DESCENDING MOON

The period when the moon is in its descending or ascending phase has a decisive effect on plant growth. But this is *not* to be confused with the waxing or waning moon, which is something different (see drawing).

In the 27 or so days in which the moon orbits the earth once, it rises from its deepest point (in the region of the Archer) to its highest point (in the region of the Twins), then descends again from its highest to its lowest point.

As the moon is descending the earth breathes in, and all forces pass to the root. That is why this time is propitious for planting out, planting bulbs and root vegetables.

As the moon is ascending the earth breathes out again, and forces concentrate on growth above ground. This is, for instance, the time to take cuttings, and to harvest fruit for storage.

Seeds can be sown both during ascending and descending moon, but one should avoid unfavourable constellations caused by the moon or planets.

Planting time (right) and non-planting time (left). Planting and sowing is done during the time of the descending moon. When the moon is ascending, scions are cut and apples harvested

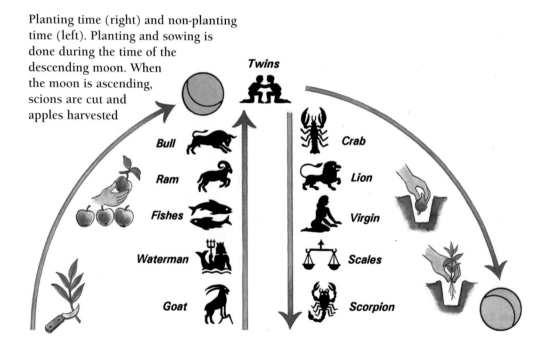

8

THE COURSE OF THE DAY

Within a single day, too, various forces are at work. Until midday ascending forces are active, and after noon descending forces come into play. Here are some examples.

Radishes harvested in the morning retain fresh leaves for a long time but the roots themselves quickly go limp. By waiting until evening before fetching them from the soil, we get a solid and firm 'fruit' which lasts much longer.

Lettuce keeps a fresher head for a long time if we harvest it in the morning. Harvested after midday and in the afternoon, in contrast, it quickly goes limp, and we have to use it up immedi-

ately. And it also loses up to 10% of its weight.

Animals also experience this rhythm. For instance, we were told about Indian elephants who carted around heavy tree trunks and loads without a problem until around 11.30 a.m., but refused to do such work any later than this. We therefore assume that animals have access to greater strength as the day 'rises' than when it is 'sinking' again.

Pictured here is a carrot trial: we harvested the seeds from sowings at various constellations to see how cultivation times affect further generations

THE GROUND RULES

Below we have compiled nine important ground rules for you:

Top: In this trial we planted rose cuttings on leaf days during the planting period. The cuttings quickly rooted but initially developed no flowers

Bottom: A quite different picture arises if cuttings are planted during the planting period on blossom days with the moon in Twins. They blossom very quickly, and later in abundance

Rule 1: Root plants are tended on root days. In other words, sowing, planting out, all hoeing and cultivation work as well as harvesting and preserving take place on root days.

Rule 2: Leaf plants are sown, planted out and cultivated on leaf days. Fruits for storage are harvested on blossom days. Everything for immediate use, e.g. lettuce, is taken fresh from the garden at any time.

Rule 3: Blossom plants are sown, planted out and harvested on blossom days.

Rule 4: Fruit plants are sown, planted out, hoed and cultivated on fruit days. Fruit days should also be chosen for harvesting and preserving.

Rule 5: It is best to plant and sow at the period of descending moon (planting period). At this time the plant's forces accumulate in the parts of the plant below ground. Plants therefore root and grow well.

Rule 6: All work that draws on the forces found in the parts of the plant above ground, e.g. taking cuttings, is best done during the period of the ascending moon (i.e. not the planting period).

Rule 7: If it proves impossible to sow plants on the best days for them, it is important to undertake all other cultivation work at favourable times.

Rule 8: If you want to harvest seeds for the following year, then choose fruit days for sowing, hoeing, cultivation and harvest of fruit plants. If you need the seeds of leaf plants, then it is best to sow, hoe and cultivate the plants on leaf days until they have reached the stage of full development. All subsequent work should then be done on fruit days instead. It is very important only to collect seeds from plants that have grown into very healthy, well-developed specimens. If you ignore this rule you are likely, for instance, to get only small, misshapen heads of lettuce the following year.

Rule 9: If fruits or leaves are collected in the wild, we are guided by the following rules. Harvest roots and bark on root days, leaves and blossoms on blossom days, and fruit and seeds on fruit days. Dry everything in an airy, well-shaded place – and never use electrical appliances, as we have found this diminishes the aroma. The dry plants are stored in bags or glass jars with cork stoppers. We never use metal storage jars.

Onion trials: we harvest the seeds from these plants to see how different sowing days will affect the next generation of plants the following year

Effects on plant growth

In numerous trials over many years we have found that we get the best yield and quality from plants by following these rules. For instance, lettuce will have markedly fewer leaves if we sow it during Waterman (blossom) or Ram (fruit). Lettuce sown on blossom or fruit days will have the tendency to go to seed, and therefore forms a thick stem from its root base, which depletes the leaf mass.

11

GOOD FRIDAY AND EASTER SATURDAY

From Good Friday to Easter Saturday we do no work in the garden at all. In numerous trials we have repeatedly found that garden work of any kind during this period, including harvest, does plants and people no good. Fewer seeds germinate, fruits are smaller, produce quality is diminished and medicinal herbs have less healing power. However we ponder this question, ultimately we always come back to the conviction that the cosmic event at Golgotha penetrated and imbued the earth, and plants annually participate in this.

This trial clearly shows that gardening work should be left alone on Good Friday and Easter Saturday. We harvested dandelion blossoms and stinging nettles from Good Friday to Easter Monday. Everything was dried and then we made teas from the herbs, and with them watered wheat grains planted in flower pots. Very few of the seeds that had been watered with teas harvested on Good Friday and Easter Saturday germinated

MARIA THUN'S SOWING CALENDARS

This trial demonstrated the influence of a transit of Mercury over the sun – something that only happens every eleven years. The result: only a few seeds germinated during the transit, but by 8 p.m. in the evening the event had passed and all the radish seeds germinated

Since 1963 we have been publishing our own calendar,* which enables gardeners and farmers throughout the world to cultivate fruit, vegetables and grains according to this method. This booklet provides all the information you need to make use of the positive effects of moon, stars and planets on plant growth in your garden.

It is important to note that it is not just the moon but also many other occurrences in the cosmos which radically affect plants, for example eclipses or nodes. The planets also have a great effect both on the weather and on plant growth. For instance, if Venus, a light/air planet, passes in front of a light/air constellation such as the Twins, we are likely to have a clearer, bluer sky, greater amounts of sunshine, and a clearer atmosphere.

---

*Sowing and planting calendar available in the UK from Floris Books (see address at back of book).

Kohlrabi sown during a Mars eclipse typically divide into a cross shape

Our allocations

Zodiac sign	Element	Planets and sun
Ram, Lion, Archer	Warmth	Mercury, Saturn, Pluto
Bull, Virgin, Goat	Earth	Sun
Twins, Scales, Waterman	Air/light	Venus, Jupiter, Uranus
Crab, Scorpion, Fishes	Water	Moon, Mars, Neptune

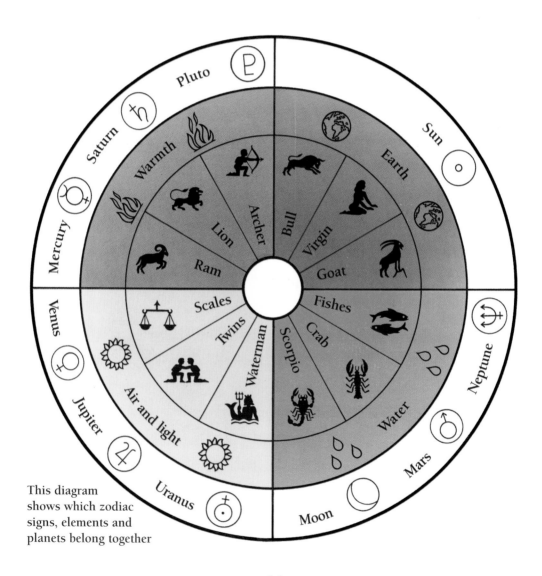

This diagram shows which zodiac signs, elements and planets belong together

OUR PREPARATIONS

In this method of cultivation, in addition to the compost preparations (see section on these below), the cow-pat pit (barrel), horn manure and horn silica preparations are also of decisive importance. Biodynamic gardening is really unthinkable without the last two.

With all three preparations you will need to sieve the mixture before applying. A mesh of double nylon stocking is perfect for this, and will prevent the spray nozzle getting blocked.

In the tips throughout this book you will frequently find references to the use of these three preparations, so here, first, is a little more about them.

HORN MANURE AND HORN SILICA PREPARATIONS

You can order both preparations from the address at the back of the book. It would be far too laborious for gardeners to make these themselves, and it might be hard, anyway, to get hold of the necessary ingredients, such as a cow horn or translucent quartz crystal — which, wherever possible, should not be adulterated by any other substances.

We make the horn silica preparation from this quartz crystal

The horn manure preparation ('500' preparation)

The 500 preparation is sprayed before sowing

This preparation is sprayed on the soil just before sowing. It promotes better root growth and thus creates the right conditions for healthy, strong plant growth. We also apply it when planting or transplanting, especially if forced to do so during the non-planting period. The preparation also promotes new root growth and should never be sprayed at the wrong time.

How it's done: Stir 3 g of horn manure preparation into 2 litres of water. This quantity is sufficient for 250 sq. m. Only one person should stir, for about an hour, getting a good vortex to form (see drawing on page 17). Use the preparation within the next four hours, as after that it loses its efficacy.

Application: Spray on the soil three times at ten-minute intervals, directly before sowing or planting.

The horn silica preparation ('501' preparation)

Horn silica is sprayed on plants while they are growing, and again the right days must be chosen (i.e. leaf plants such as lettuce on leaf days, fruit plants such as tomatoes on fruit days). This treatment keeps plants healthy and leads to better harvests and greater quality of produce.

How it's done: Stir 0.5 g of the preparation into 4 to 5 litres of water for about an

16

hour. Take care to create a good vortex (see drawing). For 100 sq. m you will need 0.5 litres of spraying fluid. The stirred preparation must be used within the next four hours, as after that it loses its efficacy.

It is important to create a good vortex when stirring both the horn manure and horn silica preparations, so that cosmic forces can be fully 'sucked in' and integrated. Therefore one only stirs outside in the open air. Once a vortex has properly formed, we remove the wooden stick, allow the fluid to continue circling for a moment, and then stir again in the opposite direction

Use of the silica preparation

Group	Spraying time (directly on plants)
Root plants	On root days: three times a month, so roughly every nine days, in the morning after sunrise
Leaf plants	On leaf days: three times a month, after sunrise
Blossom plants	On blossom days: three times a month, after sunrise
Fruit/seed plants	On fruit/seed days: three times a month, after sunrise

THE COW-PAT PIT (BARREL) PREPARATION

My son Matthias ploughing. The cow-pat pit (barrel) and horn manure preparations are sprayed from the tractor at the same time as the ground is cultivated, thus saving the farmer time. The two preparations work best when the soil is agitated at the same time as spraying

I like having lots of flowers growing around the house. Here I'm planting asters in a window box

It is very laborious to make the cow-pat pit (barrel) preparation yourself, and this is only really worthwhile for farmers or professional gardeners with big acreages. The amateur gardener can order it, along with instructions for use (see addresses at back of book).

The cow-pat pit (barrel) preparation stimulates the life of the soil, ensuring better and quicker transformation and breakdown of organic and mineral substances. We spray it once when manure or compost is applied to beds, or when a green manure is dug in.

The cow-pat pit (barrel) preparation counteracts radioactivity in the soil. For example, local authorities found that following the Chernobyl disaster many soils were free of radioactivity if treated regularly with this preparation.

Making the cow-pat pit (barrel) preparation

Take five 10-litre buckets of cow manure (from cows on a biodynamic farm that have been on a roughage diet for a few days), 100 g of dry, finely ground eggshells (from a biodynamic farm) and 500 g basalt sand (0.2 to 0.5 mm grain size). All of this is placed in a wooden vat and stirred about (dynamized) for an hour. After this, in the open air, we put half of it into a wooden container without a bottom that has been sunk 40 to 50 cm deep in the earth. The earth that has been removed for this purpose is heaped up around the barrel. Now we add a half portion of compost preparations to this as arranged in the compost heap (see drawing on page 20), and then put the other half of the mixture into the barrel, followed by the other portion of compost preparations in the same arrangement. Next, stir five drops of valerian preparation in a litre of water for ten minutes, and pour over the contents of the barrel. Finally close the barrel with a wooden lid. After leaving it for four weeks it is stirred around briefly, and after another four weeks it is ready to use.

How to use the cow-pat pit (barrel) preparation

Stir 6 g of cow-pat pit (barrel) preparation in 2 litres of water. Whereas the horn manure and horn silica preparations should be stirred for an hour, the cow-pat pit mixture only needs to be stirred for 20 minutes and can then be used over the next four days, in contrast to the other two preparations whose effect only lasts for four hours. The cow-pat pit preparation is sprayed three times in autumn or spring.

Application: We spray this on three consecutive days, at the same time as manure or green manure is applied, once in November, and twice in March once the ground is free of frost. We also use the cow pat pit preparation for our fruit trees (see page 77).

The cow-pat pit (barrel) preparation is very important in our method of cultivation, and has a highly beneficial effect on the life of the soil. We also found that regular use dispels radioactivity from the soil

19

BIODYNAMIC COMPOST PREPARATIONS

Preparations made from six herbs are added to biodynamic compost, as you can see from the drawing below. These preparations are made from yarrow, camomile, stinging nettle, oak bark, dandelion and valerian. In trials with these preparations we added very small quantities of them to plant soils and found very big differences in appearance and yield in all the plants thus treated.

To discover how teas made from these preparation plants affect cultivated plants, we examined these herbs in greater detail.

Yarrow: Rudolf Steiner stresses the special action of sulphur. He says that its

Five holes measuring about 50 cm are dug in a heap of biodynamic compost, and the preparations (made of camomile, yarrow, dandelion, stinging nettle and oak bark) are inserted into the heap

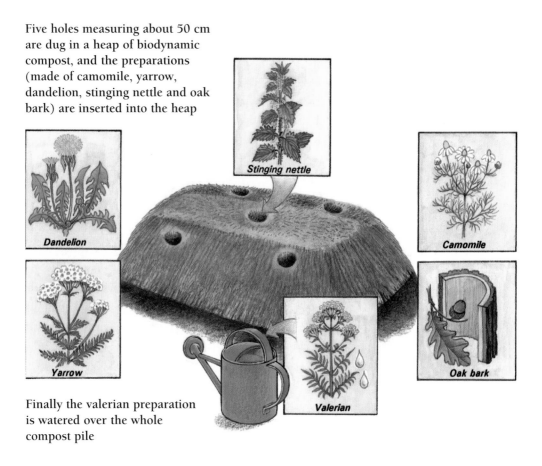

Dandelion

Stinging nettle

Camomile

Yarrow

Valerian

Oak bark

Finally the valerian preparation is watered over the whole compost pile

effect in yarrow is to stimulate the potassium process in organisms. We know that a deficiency of potassium activity can lead to radioactive caesium being deposited in organisms.

Camomile: In nature camomile grows on compacted soils that can turn to mud. If we pull up a specimen the root smells of a mixture of sulphur and carbon dioxide. Rudolf Steiner considers that camomile naturally develops the potassium process in the right way. At the same time it has also mastered the carbon process. During the war camomile was used to combat epidemics of diarrhoea.

Stinging nettle: As a young girl I learned that stinging nettles are particularly good for geese (see page 50). Many people like eating stinging nettles as a wild vegetable. It seems to have a positive effect on our iron, potassium and magnesium balance. Rudolf Steiner called the stinging nettle an 'all-rounder', and speaks of it in connection with sulphur, potassium, calcium and its iron content. My grandmother used to make a stinging nettle tea once a week to wash her hair in – it is said to help combat sparse hair growth.

Oak bark: To make this compost preparation one needs the bark of old trees. For bee feed and to make a tea, a piece of bark from the common oak or the sessile oak is placed in cold water and boiled up for 15 minutes. Allow to cool before use.

Dandelion: This plant, which many lawn-lovers regard as a blemish on their green carpet, plays an important role in

Purely plant composts are suitable for all plants which don't like animal manures, such as onions and carrots

View of our long lines of compost in the valley field

21

Biodynamic compost

We use the six compost preparations (above). To introduce them into the compost, holes are made in the heap according to a predetermined arrangement (see drawing on page 20), and the preparations are then inserted into these. Finally we water the whole heap with the valerian preparation (right)

natural remedies and is also used as wild salad.

The flowers should be harvested before the bees visit them, so you have to observe when the blossoms open for the first time, in the morning, and gather them before the inner blossom has opened.

This is how dandelion flowers should look at the best harvesting time

MULCHING AND GREEN MANURING

By mulching we mean covering the soil with organic material, but at the same time we also want to add additional organic substance to the earth and activate the soil's life. Green manuring means cultivating the so-called green manure plants such as tansy or phacelia, lupins and mustard, and later digging them into the soil.

In our trials we have repeatedly found that the planting period is of particular significance for soil formation. If green manure plants are dug in during this time, the soil's organisms immediately begin their work and convert the fresh organic material into substances that plants can access.

The same also holds good for mulching. At the planting period the soil's organisms quickly draw the mulch into the earth and transform it. At other times grass placed on the soil quickly goes dry and serves only as ground cover, but nevertheless still has a positive effect on soil life.

The best green manure

By choosing the right plant you can give your soil what it lacks.

If nitrogen and calcium are lacking, it is best to choose green manure plants such as clover, lupins, peas and lentils.

Phacelia, cornflower, corn-cockle and flax activate phosphorus in the soil. Borage and buckwheat introduce potassium.

If grains are to grow on a bed, it is good to plant rape, mustard or oilseed radish as green manure. These three plants excrete sulphurous substances which lead to higher yields in grains.

The 500 preparation stimulates more nitrogen nodules

CROP ROTATION

One frequently reads that the rhythm governing crop rotation should be: heavy feeder, medium feeder, light feeder. We have a slightly different view from this.

Firstly we take care to change the plant family. Plants from the same species should never be cultivated directly after one another on the same plot of ground. Many pests attack all the members of one family, and related plants often drain the soil of nutrients in a one-sided way. Take care, particularly, with the brassica family, which includes many vegetables: cabbages, red and white radish, kohlrabi, Brussels sprouts and cauliflower. Another factor is that plants naturally pass through the five stages of root, leaf, blossom, seed, fruit, and wish to 'realize' themselves in the soil. In practice we see a fourfold division of root, leaf, blossom, fruit/seed. This means that for each bed we choose, in succession, a root plant, a leaf plant, a blossom plant and a fruit plant. Try to draw up a crop rotation plan according to this fundamental sequence. A list of plants belonging to each group can be found at the back of this book. Don't forget to include green manure plants in the rotation sequence.

We plant lettuces, red orache, endive, lamb's lettuce and spinach as an inter-crop between the different rotation stages, and this has never yet given rise to any rotation problems. Despite this they shouldn't follow one another in a single year.

Examples for several years

Year 1	Year 2	Year 3	Year 4	Year 5
Broccoli	Beetroot	Bush beans	Potatoes	Strawberries
Red radish	Parsley	Tomato	Flowers	Strawberries
Long radish	Leaf herbs	Pepper	Jerusalem artichoke	Strawberries
Long radish	Parsley	Cucumber	Flowers	Strawberries
Cauliflower	Beetroot	Bush beans	Broccoli	Strawberries

A crop rotation that has proved successful with us is: long radish (top left), parsley (top right), cucumber (above left), flowers (above right) and, in year five, strawberries (bottom right)

THE SOIL'S PH VALUE

Unfortunately we often have to struggle with acidic soil, sometimes so acidic that vegetables and grains cannot grow successfully.

On one very acidic plot we found we could raise the pH value from 5 to 5.8 if we sprayed the soil with herbal teas. By using the horn manure preparation we achieved a value of 6.1. The cow-pat pit (barrel) preparation raised this still further to 6.8.

This is a quite astonishing result. By using these treatments, therefore, we can make every soil capable of cultivation.

MAKING YOUR OWN TEAS FOR PLANT HEALTH

Home-made plant teas strengthen our plants against disease and provide higher yields. The teas are always sprayed cold onto plants

Blossoms and herbs are drying on these fruit racks

Oak bark for making herbal teas. These are sprayed cold

For plant teas we use valerian, stinging nettle, dandelion, oak bark, yarrow and camomile. All the teas are sprayed over the plant and strengthen it against pests, and also give better quality and yield.

For yarrow, camomile, dandelion and valerian we add 1 g of dried blossoms to 10 litres of water. Boiling water is poured over the blossoms, and after 15 minutes they are sieved. The fluid must be cold before use.

For stinging nettle we add 5 g of dried leaves to 10 litres of water, boil briefly and then sieve after 15 minutes and allow to cool. One can also make the tea with 1 litre of water, and later add another 9 litres.

Horsetail (equisetum) and oak bark must be added to cold water, boiled up for 15 minutes, and then sieved and allowed to cool. Take 1 g horsetail per ten litres water, and 5 g of oak bark. Once the tea is cold, it is sprayed through a fine nozzle. Ten litres of spray fluid are enough for $\frac{1}{4}$ hectare (2500 sq. m). Since only a little is used in the garden, you only need to prepare a little: 1 litre is sufficient for 250 sq. m.

EARLY SPRING AND SPRING

COUNTRY PROVERBS

For farmers and gardeners there are a few important country sayings which many adhere to. The best-known in Central Europe are the Ice Saints, or Frost Saints, from 12 to 15 May: St Pancras on the 12th, St Servatius on the 13th, St Boniface on the 14th, and finally the so-called Cold Sophia on the 15th. Many wait until this time has passed before putting out pots and tubs on terraces or balconies, because no further frost is expected.

In various trials we found that several weather proverbs no longer apply to the old, traditional dates. This is understandable as the position of the sun shifts by one degree every 72 years, which equates to a whole day. A country saying that dates back 700 years would already have shifted by 10 days.

Unfortunately we haven't yet had time to test the most important country proverbs from this perspective. But we have made observations for a few, which you can read about below and on pages 54–5.

Candlemas

An old English saying for Candlemas, on 2 February, goes:

If Candlemas be fair and bright,
Come, Winter, have another flight;
If Candlemas brings clouds and rain,
Go Winter, and come not again.

In European tradition if a hedgehog comes out on this day and sees his

A view of our field trials

shadow because the sun is shining, he gets a fright and hurries back to his burrow for another six weeks.

According to our observations, Candlemas nowadays falls on 15 February. Accordingly, the saying must be about 950 years old, i.e. date back to 1050. We also know that in those days the sun stood in Waterman on 2 February. And if the sun stands in Waterman then it is a time likely to be especially favoured by light. Today the sun only stands in Waterman from 14 February, which supports our views.

It's lovely when the gardening season starts again. The first lettuce leaves are soon ready for picking

St Joseph's Day

St Joseph's Day on 19 March is said to be good for taking cuttings. We found that cuttings taken on this day only do well when it is also the planting period. At other times cuttings do not root particularly well, not even on St Joseph's Day.

The Ice Saints

For decades we have found that when, in May, the moon and the planets stand in zodiac signs that have an effect on the element of earth, certain angular positions can give rise to night frosts. Sometimes such constellations fall on the dates of the Ice Saints, but also, often, on other dates too.

Ascension Day

Ascension Day used to be a very important day for gathering various wild plants. In the late afternoon and at twilight we had to go out to pick leaves of coltsfoot, woodruff, lily of the valley, lady's mantle, silverweed and the young shoots of willow, birch, wild rose, hazelnut and spruce. All parts of these plants were dried on paper in the attic of the house. Once dried, it was all placed in a special room. Sometimes we opened the door of this room simply to breathe in the wonderful, intense aroma of the herbs.

IN THE GREENHOUSE

Just 14 days after planting lettuce we plant the young tomato plants. These two neighbours don't trouble one another. Before the tomatoes start taking light from the lettuce it will have been harvested

We have a small greenhouse in which we start planting early in the year – lettuce, kohlrabi, red radishes and leaf herbs, all sown in pots. Lettuce is planted in the bottom bed. We start the first sowings from the end of February, and when the first freshly pulled lettuce appears on the table in April it is always a moment for celebration.

We heat the greenhouse only for a short period in early spring if we want to sow lettuce in February. Cauliflower and kohlrabi sowings at the beginning of March are aided with electrical heat.

In the greenhouse we also cultivate chicory, which in winter supplies our table with additional vitamins (see page 73).

Lettuce plants in our small greenhouse. They are followed by tomatoes and cucumbers

In the greenhouse we start sowing lettuce as early as possible

The greenhouse is the ideal place to bring on tomatoes, sweet peppers, aubergines and chillies. Later – after the Ice Saints – we move all these plants outside. Of course, you can continue to grow vegetables in the greenhouse.

Straw bales in the greenhouse

Soil diseases can develop in the greenhouse due to repeated planting of the same types of vegetable, and the difficulty of keeping to a crop rotation plan. We can overcome this problem by using straw bale cultivation.

To do this we fetch straw bales, cut them open but leave them as whole bales. In the middle a trough is excavated and mature compost is placed inside this. Into this one plants cucumbers or tomatoes. The best kind of straw to use is oat straw.

Plant cucumbers in straw bales to avoid crop rotation problems in the smaller greenhouse

Other types can be used but are not so good. Wheat straw has greater warmth forces than barley. Rye straw has a high silica content. After harvesting, the rotting straw can go on the compost heap.

Tomatoes can also be planted in straw bales

33

TIPS FOR SPECIFIC PLANTS

Lettuce grows better like this

Immediately before planting out, we nip the ends of the longer roots of young lettuce plants

If our lettuce sowings are sufficiently large that the seedlings need more space or can be planted outside, we nip the ends of the longer roots. This gives rise to better forking and more roots. The plants grow better and the lettuce heads get bigger.

We actually used to do the same thing whenever cabbage or sugar beet were planted out in the fields. Nipping off the ends of the roots with one's fingers was just a natural hand movement that belonged to the process, something we did as a matter of course.

For the best harvest and healthy heads, lettuce must be sown, thinned, transplanted and hoed on leaf days.

Lettuce's favourite teas

Our tests were able to show that both seed development and head formation were positively affected by tea infusions. Lettuce loves teas made of yarrow, oak bark and valerian (preparing teas, see pages 26–7).

Healthy pumpkins on one of our trial fields

A few varieties — some recommendations

For cauliflower we have had good results with the 'Erfurter Zwerg' variety. For early lettuce we choose 'May King', and for later, 'Brauner Trotzkopf', 'Attrazione' (also called 'White Boston') and 'Neckarperle'. All these varieties respond very positively to biodynamic methods of cultivation.

Large lamb's lettuce plants

We sow lamb's lettuce in April and May already, which prevents it going to seed, and individual plants thicken up very well. This means that new plantlings keep forming at the root stock, giving rise to especially big plants. Lamb's lettuce belongs to the leaf plants, and sowing and cultivation measures are therefore carried out on leaf days.

'Super Green' spinach responds well to our cultivation methods

Lamb's lettuce all the year round

We can harvest fresh lamb's lettuce almost all the year round. For summer use we sow in April and May. In July, August and September we make regular further sowings, which can also be harvested over winter.

'Super Green' — our top-notch spinach

We rarely grow spinach beet. We love spinach. About 40 years ago I received a wonderful variety called 'Super Green' from Denmark. This makes big, tasty leaves, and we consider it the best type of all. Since then we have not only harvested plenty of spinach but also make sure we get enough seed for the next year.

Spinach trials

When we sow spinach on a blossom day the plant forks a great deal (left). Sowing on fruit days means that the plants run to seed quickly (second from left). When seeds are sown on leaf days this produces the best plants (second from right). Sowing on root days produces measly specimens (right)

Parsley

Parsley loves a soil rich in humus without additional fertilizer. It is sown, transplanted and cultivated on leaf days, which produces vital and very aromatic plants. We use parsley as a garnish with beans, cucumber, potatoes and tomato salad. We don't add it to leaf salads as its aroma doesn't suit them so well. For winter we preserve parsley in salt, and therefore can keep eating it throughout the cold winter period. You will find the precise directions for this on pages 83–6.

Proper cultivation of culinary herbs

Many herbs react sensitively to manuring. The best thing is to use pure plant compost in the autumn. Animal manures impede their fine aroma. Adding the cow-pat pit (barrel) preparation to the compost will support soil life. In spring we spray once with horn manure, and again after every cutting. Leaf herbs are sprayed with horn silica on leaf days. For a high etheric oil content we give horn silica on blossom days.

The right tea for cress

Since cress only has a very short growth period we only spray the soil with various teas, never the leaves themselves. We have found that cress responds best to yarrow and horsetail teas (for preparation, see pages 26–7).

Cress is all the healthier for teas. The soil in which germinated seedlings are growing is sprayed with the tea

Fresh radishes

We start our radishes in the greenhouse in March, and the first ones are ready for harvesting four to six weeks later. We sow continually until the end of September. Then, sadly, we have to wait five months until April of the following

Here you can see that radishes from different sowings have developed differently. In front grow well-developed radishes, behind are more atypical ones. We leave these 'good and bad' plants standing, collect the seed, and sow them again the following year, to see how the next generation grows

year. It is important to remember that radishes are root plants, and so they should be sown and cultivated on root days.

Red radishes love camomile, valerian and oak bark

If you want to do your radishes a good turn, give them a tea made of camomile, valerian and oak bark. We found that treating them with stinging nettle gave the greatest leaf growth, whereas the radish root is improved when sprayed with camomile. We obtained the best seeds by spraying with camomile, oak bark and valerian teas (see pages 26–7 for tea preparation).

Kohlrabi also has its favourite tea

In the case of kohlrabi we want a solid but not woody 'fruit' to form. We obtained the best results by giving teas made of dandelion, yarrow and stinging nettle (see pages 27–7 for tea preparation).

Teas for cauliflower

Of all treatments, cauliflower showed that it preferred stinging nettle and oak bark sprayed over its leaves (see pages 26–7 for tea preparation).

Red radishes with seeds, in front; behind, flowering lettuces

Cabbage preferences

The cabbages – with the exception of broccoli – belong to the leaf plants, and so we sow them on leaf days after a brief prior application of horn manure preparation. Once small seedlings have developed, we prick them out into soil that has also been sprayed with horn

37

Best inner quality and outer appearance in kohlrabi was obtained when it was sown on leaf days, e.g. Moon in Crab

manure. Before planting out we once again spray the soil with horn manure. It is important to do this on leaf days during the planting period.

Once the young plants have developed new leaves, we start spraying them with horn silica, three times at intervals of nine or ten days, in the early mornings on leaf days. This gives the plants a better aroma and produces a higher yield.

In the case of cabbages for storing, and for making sauerkraut, we spray the silica preparation about three weeks before harvest, in the morning on blossom days (!), rather than on leaf days. For more about making sauerkraut see pages 89–92.

By cultivating cabbage according to our methods we avoid root disease altogether, and can harvest the finest heads

Carrots like following rye

Carrots should not be sown on beds that have been treated with compost in the autumn. They prefer a devitalized soil. We have found, otherwise, that the carrot fly becomes more of a problem. We obtained the best results when carrots were sown where grain had grown previously, particularly rye.

Carrots like following rye in the crop rotation sequence

The 'Rothild' variety of carrot is particularly suitable for our cultivation methods

Winter carrots and the Bull sun

In all our tests we found that carrots for winter storage like being sown on root days after 13 May, once the sun passes into the Bull constellation.

Plants develop best at this time and grow very fast. We obtained very good results with the 'Rothild' variety, the winter carrot variety we plant most often. It responds very well to biodynamic cultivation.

In trials we found very low nitrate levels and very high sugar content in the juice from our carrots. This is due to the horn silica preparation and our spraying of herbal teas.

Carrots and parsnips

Carrots and parsnips sown, hoed and harvested on root days remain healthy. It is also very important not to let the young plants stand too close together. It is better to thin them a little now and then.

Sun Bull

We had the best results with our favourite 'Rothild' carrot variety when we sowed it with the sun in the Bull, and the moon in root signs

Sowing comparisons: the carrots on the right and left were sown on Mercury node days; the carrots in the middle were sown on root days and show typical root formation

'Paris Market' and 'Nantaise'

We have obtained excellent results with the two (non-storing) carrot varieties 'Paris Market' ('Parmex', 'Parabel') and 'Nantaise'. We sow them on root days during the planting period at the end of April, directly into the soil. All cultivation measures are also carried out on root days.

If children refuse carrots

If your children don't like carrots, try to serve them on root days. In our experience this gets over the problem! According to the nutritionist and researcher Dr Renzenbrink, children like eating them on those days.

The best soil preparation for potatoes

An old proverb says that potatoes should be treated with manure in spring so that the plant grows quickly. We do not do this. In numerous trials we repeatedly found that, even for the potato, compost and well-rotted manure must be worked into the soil in advance, in the autumn — during the planting period in the month of October. At the same time we spray the cow-pat pit (barrel) preparation, and after about four weeks — though no later than mid-November — we plough the winter furrow. This enables soil organ-isms to work best, and after mid-November to be left undisturbed in their work.

In spring the soil is then cultivated again and the horn manure preparation is sprayed. The potatoes are planted on root days and, since they love air getting to their tubers, we hoe twice on root days and give the silica preparation at the same time. At the third hoeing, too, we spray with silica. If the potatoes are not planted on raised banks, they will need to be earthed up after about four weeks so that the tubers don't turn green.

Healthy potatoes

Potatoes can be very well protected from *Phytophthora* (blight). Once the second pair of leaves has unfurled, spray them with stinging nettle tea on a leaf day evening. Then, at nine-day intervals, spray them on root day mornings with a succession of yarrow, camomile, dandelion and stinging nettle — in this specific order.

It is also very important to plant and hoe them on root days, and as we mentioned in the 'tips', to spray them with the silica preparation three times on root days. You will not lose any plants if you do this.

We don't plant early potatoes since we can fetch good, healthy potatoes from storage right up to August (see page 83).

Cultivating potatoes

1. Work in compost in the autumn, and spray the cow-pat pit preparation twice.
2. Plant potatoes on root days in spring
3. Spray the silica preparation and hoe on root days, three times in succession

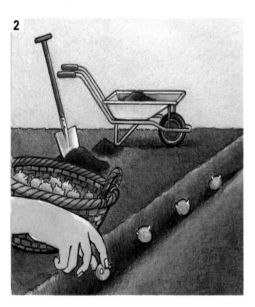

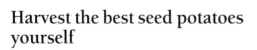

Harvest the best seed potatoes yourself

To raise the best seed potatoes we plant them when the sun and moon are in the Ram. Nowadays the sun is in the Ram in the period between 18 April and 12 May. The moon passes into this constellation at a different time each year, and you can look it up each year in our planting and sowing calendar. Seed potatoes need to be planted more

Potato trial: We planted potatoes on various days; those planted on blossom days developed blossoms quickly whereas those planted on root days bloomed much later, which is desirable

closely together, so that the tubers remain smaller.

Broccoli loves blossom days

One could easily assume that broccoli is a leaf plant. However, trials have repeatedly shown that this vegetable belongs to the blossom plants, and should therefore be sown, transplanted, hoed and cultivated on blossom days.

If you do this broccoli will grow very healthily, pests will not be a problem, and you will get the highest yields.

Sow broad beans early

The broad bean — a vegetable we are very fond of — is one of the fruit plants. It can be sown as soon as the soil is no longer frozen, preferably on fruit days when the sun is in Waterman (between 14 February and 10 March).

Peas, runner beans and bush beans

In our climate we cannot sow peas in the open until the end of April. They should be sown on fruit days.

We can greatly increase the yield of peas by spraying the horn silica preparation on fruit days. Doing the same on leaf days gave rise to markedly reduced yields.

You can see clearly from these two photos that broccoli belongs to the blossom plants. Top left a lovely 'single head' from sowing on blossom days; bottom left a strongly forking plant from a leaf day sowing

Beans are sensitive to frost and are only sown in May after all danger of frost has passed.

Sweetcorn loves fertile soil

Sweetcorn, a fruit plant, is sown in May, but not too early. Choose fruit days for sowing. To get a good harvest the soil must be rich. We add compost to the beds in the autumn — two bucketfuls of mature compost per square metre (see pages 70–1).

Sunflower, rapeseed and linseed

We get the best growth and highest seed yield from oil fruits when we sow them on fruit days. If we want to obtain oil from them, it is advisable to hoe and spray with silica on blossom days. The oil yield will then be greater.

For larger-scale field trials we sow by machine

Planting vine cuttings

In various tests we tried to find the best time for taking and planting cuttings. We kept finding the same thing: one should take scions in the first hours when the moon is in Twins but not yet ascending. Then one needs to store them for a few days in cool conditions, and plant them when the moon is in Lion. They will quickly form roots and develop into fine, healthy plants that bear many grapes.

A living fence

A living fence can easily be created using willow sticks. These 'cuttings' are planted crosswise, 30 cm deep in the soil during the March planting period. Shoots will quickly start growing, and soon form a dense fence or hedge.

45

We have been doing oil trials for many years. This pumpkin gives us seeds for making oil

Stinging nettle compost

The best earth for raising vegetables and herbs is obtained from pure stinging nettle compost. The important thing here is to compost only stinging nettles, and add no other organic material. Once fully broken down, this compost is excellent for cultivating roses and strawberries.

Spruce needle compost — when successfully broken down (!) — is the only other source of such good earth quality.

Sowing times for trees and shrubs

For sowing and planting the planting period is usually chosen. In addition the trees live 'with' the various planets. For instance birch, lime, robinia and larch respond to Venus and Mercury; maple, common beech, sweet chestnut and apple are influenced by Jupiter forces; the needle trees, hornbeam, blackthorn and plum take their lead from Saturn; and morello cherry, horse chestnut and

Here you can see the results of trials with vine cuttings. The cuttings in the two left-hand pots were planted on fruit days, while those in the two right-hand pots were planted on root days — in all cases during the planting period.

Only the plants in the left-hand pots rooted well, clearly showing the positive influence of fruit days

Our fence of willow cuttings in the first year

Earth composed of stinging nettle compost is excellent for roses

47

During the growing period we need all hands to cope with the work

oak have chosen Mars as their presiding planet.

For the best sowing time we choose, where possible, days when the respective planets are in opposition.

In our annual sowing and planting calendar we have compiled the best days for you.

A tip for combating ants

We frequently have a problem with ants in the greenhouse. When this happens we pour a good deal of water over the entrance places where they get in. For the house you can also place stinging nettles or nettle liquid manure where they enter. We have found that ants only thrive on soils that are poor in humus. If you have problems with these creatures, work mature compost into the soil. If they still persist, water frequently with nettle liquid manure, which ants really dislike.

Ants are often called nature's police. They consume dead animals down to the bones. Sometimes one can observe that they are too impatient to wait for death, and attack small and weakened animals before they die.

In the greenhouse ants can sometimes become a real nuisance

Proud mother goose with her five little goslings

A tip for geese rearers

As a young girl my father showed me the importance of stinging nettles. Our pair of geese were called Lieschen and Johann. After four weeks of sitting on the eggs with Johann standing guard, their numerous golden offspring made them proud parents, and it was my job to ensure that they all kept well and safe. Apart from tending them each day, I also had to collect a basketful of nettles. These were fed to the baby geese – finely cut by hand in the first few weeks, then later more roughly with the straw cutter. They ate until their crops were stuffed full, and they all stayed healthy and grew well.

SUMMER

SPECIAL DAYS IN SUMMER

The summer is one of the loveliest of seasons. Unfortunately we often have no leisure to enjoy the warm days but have to tend our plants in the garden and the fields from morning to evening. But often the evenings are a time when we do nothing, sitting round a fire in the open and simply enjoying nature.

St John's

St John's Day (24 June) is still a very important and widely known day in the

In the summer of 1980 I was given a small basket of Mirabelle or Syrian plums. They tasted so good that I decided to dry the kernels and sow them. In the winter of 1980 the kernels were planted at six different planetary oppositions, and since then they have grown into large trees. Each year we harvest wonderful fruit of six different colours, and all of them taste excellent

gardening calendar. After 24 June asparagus and rhubarb are no longer harvested, so that the plants can gather enough strength for the following year. Rhubarb also develops acids that one should not eat.

In former times this day was very important for harvesting camomile. For three days before St John's until three days after we used to pick the flower heads – still quite healthy at that time. Just a short time after this the 'fly' would lay its eggs in the blossoms, and these developed into maggots, putting paid to the camomile's medicinal effect.

The Dog Days

There are many country sayings relating to the Dog Days between 23 July and 23 August, and it would be worth finding out if they are true. When I was young we

When it has rained and this type of mist rises in the woods, there is more rain to come

used to gather yarrow, burnet and hazelnuts during this period. Why? That's just how it was.

Dormouse Day

'Dormouse Day' in Germany (not to be confused with 'Groundhog Day' or Candlemas) is 27 June. The proverb for this day is well known: 'If it rains on Dormouse Day, the rain will hold for seven weeks more.' It is important that these seven weeks only refer to rain, and not to sunshine. In other words, if the sun shines on 27 June it will stay dry but the sun won't necessarily shine every day for seven weeks.

Harvesting on Dormouse Day

In my youth the custom was to gather the flowers of meadowsweet, lime and elder on Dormouse Day. The teas made from these blossoms were given to patients to make them sweat.

TIPS FOR SPECIFIC PLANTS

Harvesting lettuce seeds for the following year

To obtain your own seed, lettuce plants are sown, planted out and hoed on leaf days – until the plants have developed fully formed heads. Then choose the finest and largest heads, as the smaller ones are unsuitable for harvesting seed and produce only small heads again the next year.

The large heads are now hoed and further cultivated on fruit days. But leaf days should again be chosen for

Preparing for a comparison between normal sowing and sowing during planetary occultations* by the moon. The plots were 5 sq. m in size. Over four weeks we sowed continuously. During these weeks we had three occultations. The resulting yield demonstrated without doubt that times when occultations take place are unsuitable for sowing.

---

* An occultation is when the moon obscures a planet.

56

harvesting the seed to ensure large, healthy heads of lettuce the following year.

My favourite herbs

Whenever people ask me what my favourite herbs are, all sorts of herbs occur to me. But after careful consideration I have to say that my principal favourites are dill, fennel, parsley, chervil, coriander and anise.

Cabbage Whites cannot bear tomatoes

Spoiling the appetite of Cabbage White

We sow and transplant cabbage on leaf days, and also choose leaf days for all cultivation work — such as hoeing and spraying with our preparations. This ensures that the plants remain healthy but is not always enough to keep Cabbage White butterflies at arm's length. They smell the cabbage from miles away, and one fine day they're suddenly there! For this reason, as a preventive measure, we interplant an area of 200 sq. m with tomato plants. Cabbage White hate the smell of tomatoes, and prefer to seek out a different dining place. It is also worth placing broken-off tomato shoots on the beds, between cabbages.

If, despite all these efforts, you discover Cabbage White caterpillars on your beds during dry weather, you can make a wormwood tea (1 g to 5 litres of

Wormwood tea, sprayed on Cabbage White caterpillars, provides additional protection against hole damage during dry weather

water, boil for ten minutes, allow to cool, strain and use). Spray the tea directly on the caterpillars; they dislike it and disappear altogether.

Keeping cabbage healthy with teas

To strengthen cabbage and give it a good aroma, we recommend spraying teas of yarrow, camomile, nettle and dandelion blossoms once on leaf days throughout the summer (see pages 26–7). However only one tea of each kind should be sprayed on any one day.

Harvesting fine Brussels sprouts

It is often not so easy to grow good Brussels sprouts in one's garden. We

Kohlrabis from unsuitable constellations at sowing. Left, during a Mars eclipse; centre, at a Mars-Pluto opposition; right, at a Neptune eclipse

have found that Brussels sprouts don't take very kindly to too much feed, which drives everything into the leaves instead of the leaf axils where the sprouts themselves form. When this vegetable fails to thrive it is often due to excess nutrients.

Cauliflower loves rich soil

In contrast to sprouts, cauliflower needs good manuring in the autumn, otherwise it will not thrive. This type of cabbage is sown and cultivated on leaf days. We don't follow the custom of covering the 'flower' with a cabbage leaf.

Harvesting tasty carrots

Keep an eye on your carrots. If the root neck appears above the level of the soil it

needs to be covered over again, as uncovered necks go green and later don't taste good. They also tempt pests to take up residence.

Harvesting calendula (English marigold) at the right time

We have harvested calendula flowers at various times, and found that the following rules hold good: when we harvest on fruit days we stimulate the plants to form new blossoms, but these flowers keep trying to form seeds. If we pick them on leaf or root days the plant responds by forming fewer flowers. When we take the blossoms on blossom days, the plant forms numerous new flowers which do not immediately start to form seeds. So it is best to choose blossom days.

Keeping roses healthy

Many roses — particularly the floribundas — are readily susceptible to black spot, mildew and rose rust. An important condition for rose health is to undertake all cultivation work on blossom days — from planting to cutting.

A rose specialist friend of mine found that his roses remained generally healthy if he sprayed them with nettle tea while they were growing and in the autumn fed them with mature, well-rotted compost composed only of

These are Siberian cucumbers. I had brought a few seeds with me from Russia because I wanted to see how well this variety would do with us. In Siberia the summer is very short, so the fruits only have two good months from sowing to harvest. At our grounds in Dexbach we were also able to harvest the cucumbers after only two months

My granddaughter Titia trying to hide in a small bush of luxuriating roses

nettles, which he worked lightly into the soil around them.

Tomatoes love teas

In numerous trials we have found that tomatoes grow better when sprayed with teas of nettle and oak bark. Nettle tea enhances the vitamin C and sugar content in the fruits. Dandelion tea improves their subtle aroma, and yarrow tea ensures more fruits per plant.

This is how we treat our tomato plants: once they have been planted out, we spray finely dispersed nettle tea on a leaf day evening, and after this camomile and dandelion tea on blossom days (once each), followed by silica (sprayed only on the leaves) three times on fruit days. After this treatment we never have problems with pests or diseases, not even with the much-feared tomato blight (tea preparation, see pages 26–7).

The best care for strawberries

After harvest our strawberry plants are given well-rotted compost. When applying this we push back all strawberry

Tomatoes like to have their side shoots removed and to be tied up to stakes

— once in the morning and once in the afternoon.* The following spring we have to remove weeds, but nothing more is needed. We never cut back the leaves; limp and fading leaves just form a cushion for the next fruits so that they don't have to lie on the soil itself.

Our strawberry plants stay put in the same location for seven to eight years, renewing themselves with offshoots. However we don't leave the strawberries there longer than eight years as their quality and yield diminish after that.

Grains grow better with teas

We were particularly interested to see how wheat, oats and rye would respond to tea sprays. We found that winter wheat loves yarrow, stinging nettle, dandelion, valerian and horsetail.

Oats took most kindly to yarrow, stinging nettle and dandelion. They grew better and were healthier, and the yield was greater.

Summer wheat responds positively to yarrow, nettle and dandelion. For summer rye sprays made of yarrow, dandelion and nettle teas proved very effective. The plants stayed healthier and the yield was higher (for tea preparation, see pages 26–7).

tendrils into the rows and place the compost carefully alongside them, working it into the soil. This is best done on fruit days during the planting period: two bucketfuls for 10 sq. m. The compost should not touch the leaves. The spaces between the rows are hoed two or three times. On hoeing days we apply horn manure once and silica preparation twice

*The hoeing days recur every 8–9 days (fruit days). On one of these hoeing days horn manure is applied. On the next hoeing day (9 days later) horn silica is applied in the morning and on the third hoeing day (another 9 days later) horn silica is applied in the afternoon.

61

The best time to feed strawberries with compost is on fruit days after harvest during the planting period

Old seed stock

This year we had old cucumber and courgette seed stock and, like gardeners everywhere, were reluctant to throw it away. So we just tried sowing it close together. However, we shouldn't have assumed that few seeds would germinate. We could hardly believe how many did. Was it really old seed? And then the second mistake: we couldn't simply tear up the young plants, so in the end we left them standing far too close together, and overflowing into garden areas that weren't intended for them. Oh well, once the growing season has finished it will all be over — so we just left them to grow.

Recipe for sourdough rye bread

We have developed a reliable recipe for our rye bread.

Starter dough: One heaped teaspoonful of honey is stirred well into a glass containing water at a temperature of 50°C. Then we add 250 g of fine rye meal to it. We prepare this starter dough the evening before, and leave it near the oven, stove or a radiator overnight, at around 28°–30°C. The next morning we add 250 g rye meal and 250 ml of warm water or whey. In the evening a mixture of 125 g rye flour and 125 ml water is added. Everything is kept warm overnight, at 28°–30°C.

Dough: The next morning we add 1 level teaspoon of salt to 1 kg flour and knead everything together. When the dough starts rising, we form it into loaves. These

We carried out many tea trials on grains. Summer wheat responded best to teas made of yarrow, nettle or dandelion

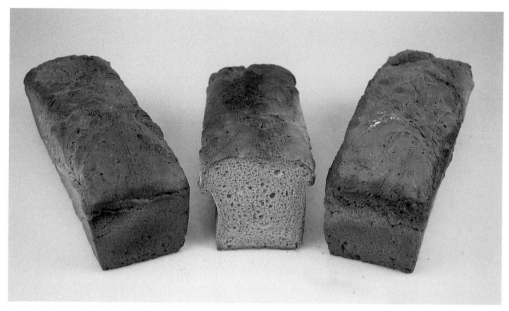

Starting bread on fruit days guarantees the best rye bread

During the summer months we have little time for leisure. We visit and check our trial fields daily

have to rise again and the next day are placed in the pre-heated oven. The loaves bake for about an hour at 200°C. Passing through these five stages, i.e. rising five times, makes the bread easily digestible. **Tip:** One can keep back about 250 g of the ready dough in a clay pot. Let it rise a little once more, wrap it up in paper and put the clay pot in a cool cellar (but not in the fridge, where it will be too cold). Then the following week you can make rye bread from it again as follows:

Mix a teaspoon of honey in a glass of warm water, add it to the dough, mix them together and place the dough

Our rye for the best rye bread. Summer rye loves teas made of yarrow, nettle or dandelion

somewhere warm. You can make the dough in the evening and when it starts to rise form it into loaves. The rest of the sequence is as described above, this time with four stages of rising.

Important: The bakery must be warm enough (28°–30°C) or the bread will not be successful.

In our experience this method is particularly successful when done on a fruit day. The overflowing dough once glued shut the door of our bakery! The moon was in front of Mars at the time. And I also found that when the moon obscured Venus the rye dough worked very well and quickly rose over the edge of the bowl – but made a very poor bread.

A portrait of beetroot

Beetroot belongs to the root plants, and is therefore sown, hoed and harvested on root days. It loves a humus-rich soil, but not manure. Spraying nettle, yarrow, dandelion and oak bark tea (in this sequence) on root days increases the yield and demonstrably improves the quality of the harvested roots.

We like eating finely grated beetroot salad, enhanced with coriander and grated apples and onions. For older people it is better to cook the beetroot beforehand. Eating this salad regularly in the winter helps prevent colds and chills.

If goats and sheep get worms we give them a special remedy made from beetroot. Plants that have been sown, hoed and harvested two days before full moon are given to the animals, again from two days before full moon until full moon. Four weeks later the process has to be repeated because of remaining eggs. Generally we have been able to rid animals of worms by this means. One can also try treating children who have worms with this method, using ordinary grated beetroot. This too should be eaten before full moon.

Our oil room. We press the oil ourselves, for instance from sunflower seeds or oilseed pumpkin. We note the different oil quantities as part of the sowing trials and investigate the contents and quality of the oil in our own laboratory

AUTUMN

THE SOIL

Preparing the soil in the right way is of course very important for the garden, since good earth is the basic precondition for rich harvests and lovely blossoms.

We add mature compost to the beds in autumn; 5 kg of well-rotted compost fits in a 10-litre bucket, and this will be enough to treat about 5 sq. m. A normal-size wheelbarrow takes a level load of 40 kg, which is enough for 40 sq. m. We recommend giving this amount every two years to maintain excellent soil fertility, and working the compost lightly into the soil.

In the spring, after the earth has dried somewhat, and about ten days before sowing or planting, the earth is worked to a depth of about 10 cm to give it a crumbly tilth.

If you wish to harvest seeds from plants it is important to keep using compost that also contains animal substances. In trials we found that lettuce stops forming good heads if fed only with plant-based composts. If one has a very weedy soil it can be cultivated when the moon is Lion. This makes the weeds germinate quickly so that they can easily be removed.

Combating weeds

1. The bed is cultivated in the spring when the moon is in Lion
2. The weeds germinate very quickly after this and can easily be removed before the crop plants are sown

We don't treat our soils with manure or compost in the spring, which has repeatedly proven to cause problems. Shoot growth is greatly stimulated when compost is applied in spring, and this attracts diseases and pests.

Important: Soils where carrots are to grow should not be given any compost (see page 39).

TIPS FOR SPECIFIC PLANTS

Harvesting wild fruits

In my childhood we used to celebrate the day of the archangel Michael, the dragon-slayer, on 29 September. After church we weren't granted any leisure, but had to go out picking wild fruits: rose hips and hawthorn, rowan, elder and juniper berries.

Walnuts, chestnuts, acorns and beechnuts could only be collected when they fell from the trees. People used to say that this happened at a different time each year because it was connected with the stars.

Sloes, on the other hand, could only be picked on St Martin's day (11 November), for it was said they only got properly sweet after a few frosty nights.

Favourable constellations when cultivating the seed-giving mother plant have a positive effect on the next generation

Endive salad can be eaten until Christmas if the plants are covered with fir branches

The last endive salad at Christmas

If you want to harvest endives as late as Christmas, then it must be sown for the last time no later than the beginning of September. The plant no longer grows after the end of November, but it can remain where it is until Christmas if covered with fir branches.

Chicory for the winter

1. October: the parts of the chicory plant above ground are cut off about 5 cm above the top of the root
2. Now cover the plants with 2 cm of earth, then straw and black plastic
3. The black plastic sheet is gradually rolled back to allow the shoots to grow

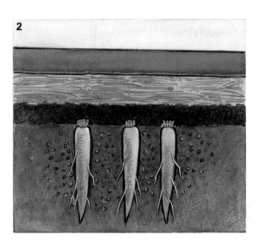

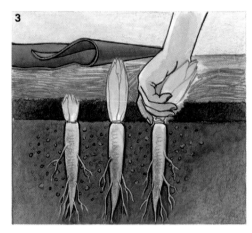

Green cabbage – healthy winter vegetable

To enhance the winter menu with fresh vegetables, we sow green cabbage in June. Green cabbage is a leaf plant and must therefore be sown, transplanted and hoed on leaf days. In October and November the green cabbage is ready to harvest, but you can also leave it until January before fetching it indoors. It tastes best after the first night frosts.

Chicory – wonderful salad almost all winter

Chicory is a rewarding winter salad that can easily be grown in the greenhouse. It is planted in an unheated greenhouse in October. The upper parts are cut back at about 5 cm from the root-top, then the plant is covered with 2 cm of earth, followed by straw and finally black plastic sheeting. After other types of salad and lettuce are over, we gradually roll back the plastic sheet and allow one plant after another to grow shoots through the straw.

Garlic

We don't grow much garlic (see also page 97) although we like the taste. Being a root plant it can be planted on root days in November and left over winter.

Onions for the following year

Onions sown in September grow into small sets by November. Then one removes them from the soil and stores them in a dry room. In spring they are planted, hoed and sprayed with silica on root days.

Jerusalem artichoke

Jerusalem artichoke develops root tubers in a way similar to the potato, and these can also be similarly used. The plant

Onions have to be quite dry before they are harvested. These ones are not quite ready

73

These onions were planted in spring during a planetary opposition. They grow into large onions which are harvested in autumn when the moon is in Lion, and are stored over winter as full-grown onions. In the second spring we plant them for seed with the moon in Lion. In this second year each one divides into eight parts, giving a large amount of seed. Unfortunately these oppositions do not occur every year around onion-planting time

belongs to the root plants, and is therefore planted and cultivated on root days. In summer, Jerusalem artichoke has beautiful blossoms that look like small sunflowers. In the autumn we harvest the tubers, but leave some in the ground so that they can grow into new plants the following year.

We prepare Jerusalem artichokes in the same way as mashed potato, and spice them with salt and, according to taste, marjoram, basil or a little nutmeg. One can also slice them into a frying pan and eat like fried potatoes.

Harvest of Jerusalem artichokes

Jerusalem artichokes develop beautiful flowers

English marigold (above), hibiscus (page 76 top), tulips (page 76 bottom) are blossom plants. Giving them compost on blossom days makes them flower profusely

Beautiful blossoms for the garden

We have found that our flowers always blossom profusely if their beds are given well-rotted compost the autumn before. It can be purely plant-based compost, since we don't want to encourage the leaves too much.

But flowers also like it when bird droppings are added to the compost (chicken and dove manure, or guano).

One just has to ensure that the compost is kept nice and moist while it breaks down, since bird manures heat up a good deal. The compost must be well rotted and have turned to earth before being spread on the beds. It is worked into the topsoil during the planting period in autumn. After a few weeks this top layer is turned under, and thus soil organisms can 'bind' the compost with the earth during the winter, giving a wonderful soil structure.

In the spring the top layer of soil is once more worked through, and sowing or transplanting can then be done on blossom days during the planting period. All other cultivation work should also be carried out on blossom days, giving a profusion of long-lasting blossoms.

Hardy flowering bulbs

Hardy flowering bulbs and tubers are planted in the autumn. Choose blossom days during the planting period, which gives health and a profusion of blossoms the following year. As long as the ground has not frozen we plant bulbs right up until December.

Dahlias and other non-hardy plants should not be planted until spring, but otherwise the same rules apply.

Protecting roses in winter

In the late autumn it is high time to give roses some protection against the cold, using fir branches. Some varieties however are more frost resistant than others. We have an energetic climbing rose on the wall of our house, which for decades now has survived the winter without any winter protection and without sustaining much damage.

The fruit year begins now

The fruit cultivation year starts for us at the beginning of November. First we treat the soil with 1000 kg of well-rotted compost per hectare. After the leaves have fallen we recommend cultivating the soil on fruit days (hoeing or rotavating) three times. At the same time the cow-pat pit (barrel) preparation should be sprayed along with application of the thinned tree paste (see page 78).

In March the horn manure preparation is sprayed three times on trunks and branches on fruit days when the ground is being cultivated.

When the first leaves unfold in spring, we spray stinging nettle tea three times on leaf days.

After blossoming, the first silica preparation spray can be applied to the leaves. We start stirring it half an hour before sunrise on a fruit day, stir for an hour and then spray it immediately.

On blossom days after this one can spray one dose of dandelion tea and one of camomile tea, and on fruit days – separately from the silica preparation – yarrow tea. During July it is good to spray the silica preparation on a fruit day one more time, to support bud formation for the following year. Summer pruning can be done on fruit days during the planting period.

Fruit for storage is harvested on blossom days or fruit days – preferably at ascending moon (non-planting period), when the moon is in Archer or Ram. After the harvest, but before the leaves fall, it is good to spray with silica on a fruit day, from 3 p.m. This helps the wood to mature and prevents fungal attack the next year.

Tree paste for fruit trees and grapevines

Cow manure and clay or loam are mixed in equal parts and stirred with whey. You can get whey from cheese-making dairies. The paste must be as thick as whitewash and is applied to trunks and thick branches with a painting brush.

Of course this mixture can also be sprayed but then you have to dilute it with water to make it very fluid. In the case of berry bushes and vines we can only spray it, not paint it on.*

---

* In his *Agriculture Course* Rudolf Steiner describes the trunk of a tree as a raised up mound of earth. The twigs and leaves then grow in this earth in a similar way to herbaceous plants growing out of the soil. Tree paste feeds and enlivens the tree bark as compost does the soil. It also helps to strengthen the plant against fungus or pest attacks.

Here we are allowing the 'Delikates' cucumber variety to ripen fully, to obtain seed

Pruning trees, bushes and hedges

If you want to cut wood you should definitely choose a day during the planting period. The parts of the tree above ground are then less full of sap. For fruit plants, such as apples or vines, fruit days should be chosen.

What can you do with green tomatoes?

Once the leaves have frozen there is no point in leaving tomatoes on the plant.

We harvest the last unripe fruits and leave them in an unheated greenhouse in a cardboard box. This usually works very well and supplies us with our own tomatoes for a few weeks longer.

Green tomatoes carry on ripening in the greenhouse

Tips for grains

I am always being asked whether there are certain days of the week when it is best to eat particular grains. There is a recommendation for this, but it should never be applied dogmatically. It won't do you any harm to eat wheat on Mondays or Tuesdays for instance.

Note: Only eat grains that have been preheated, i.e. not completely raw.

One way of eating grains on particular days of the week – not to be applied dogmatically!

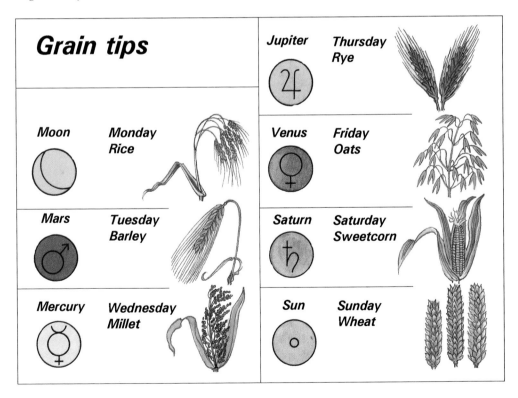

Grain tips

Moon	Monday	Rice
Mars	Tuesday	Barley
Mercury	Wednesday	Millet
Jupiter	Thursday	Rye
Venus	Friday	Oats
Saturn	Saturday	Sweetcorn
Sun	Sunday	Wheat

Sunday: wheat (sun)
Monday: rice (moon)
Tuesday: barley (Mars)
Wednesday: millet (Mercury)
Thursday: rye (Jupiter)
Friday: oats (Venus)
Saturday: sweetcorn (Saturn)
This schema gives a good spread of planetary forces in the diet.

Basic rules for storage

We never store apples in the same room as potatoes or carrots, as this is bad for the apple aroma.

Throughout the storage period diseased vegetables or fruits have to be removed regularly. A rotten apple can quickly infect the whole 'barrel'.

In the fruit cellar we store furthest forward the varieties that ripen soonest. For instance the 'Bohnapfel' apple keeps for a very long time, and is therefore placed far back in the store. In autumn it is like a stone, but wonderfully sweet in May/June.

The pear varieties 'Winterbirne' and 'Katzenkopf' keep until Whitsun, only a little before the first new early fruits appear.

We keep potatoes until August, until the next harvest is ready, and so we never grow early potatoes. We have apples, pears and potatoes all the year round.

Our valley field trial area

Here you see a hoeing and harvesting trial. As yet there is no discernible difference but in storage they behave very differently. Those hoed and harvested on root days keep for longest

Our best means of storage

Straw bales are the best way of storing fruit and vegetables. We carry bales into the barn (or attic), cut them open and take them apart. Now the 'fruits' are placed on a bed of straw and are covered with straw. Baskets and boxes can also be stored between straw. This storage method is suitable for apples, onions, carrots and white and red cabbage. You will be amazed at how good they taste.

Apples – stalk uppermost please

When storing apples on wooden shelves or trays the fruit should be laid alongside each other. It doesn't matter if they

The best means of storage: keeping fruit and vegetables in straw

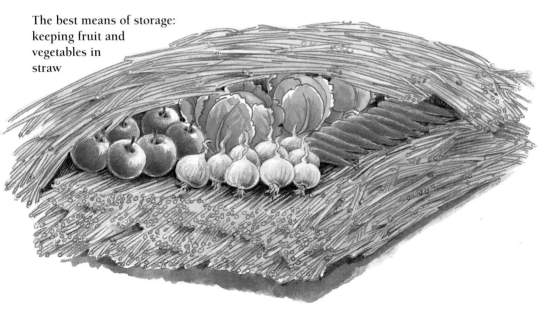

Apples and pears are stored with their stalks uppermost

touch. What does matter, though, is that the stalks should point upwards. Pears are stored in the same way.

Storing cabbages

White cabbage can also be stored in wooden trays. The plant should be harvested with a short stump, which points downwards in storage. Unfortunately cauliflower can only be stored until

November. For eating in December or later, it has to be preserved.

Brussels sprouts and green cabbage

Brussels sprouts and green cabbage can stand where they grow until spring. As we mentioned earlier, green cabbage tastes better after a few night frosts. It is harvested, depending on the state of the weather, before it grows shoots in spring, and starts to flower.

Heads of cabbage stored with their stumps downwards

Brussels sprouts can stay outside until spring

Storing bags of root vegetables on wooden shelves in a cellar

Years ago we came up with the idea of storing carrots in bags rather than in sand. The bags are permeable mesh or netting which potatoes in supermarkets often come in. It was very straightforward to store these net bags in the cellar, and easy to keep the various types of vegetable separate from each other on wooden shelves. Nowadays we put salsify roots, carrots, potatoes, celeriac and parsnips into these bags. The vegetables last a very long time and can be fetched for kitchen use in small amounts when needed.

Earth storage – yes or no?

Vegetables and fruit can be well stored in an earth store. We did this once but have absolutely decided against it. It involves a huge amount of work: digging out the store, putting in the boxes, timber over the top, putting straw into it, and earth over it. Then fetching the produce out again is a great deal of work too. The next tip shows there is another, far less laborious method.

Onion strings

Onions are stored in strings or net bags under the roof-eaves, protected from rain and snow. In our experience onions keep at temperatures down to minus 20°C. Some years we have kept onions like this very well until August of the following year.

Our herb jars

We fetch all herb plants indoors in the autumn for filling our herb jars. We put them through our mincing machine, either separately or in combinations. We add $\frac{1}{4}$ pound of salt to one pound of this

Protected outside
under the roof-eaves,
onion strings keep at
temperatures down to
minus 20°C

Many of our storage trials have shown that onions like overwintering in the open air. They just have to be protected from rain and snow

Onions fetched from storage in May. The influence of harvesting time is clear: on the left are onions harvested on root days, on the right those from blossom days

herb mass. Everything is mixed well and is placed in jars. We either seal these with a lid or close them with a linen cloth, and can use the herbs throughout the winter. We place the jars in the refrigerator or cellar so that they keep longer.

Lovage and celeriac have to be kept separate from other herbs, as their strong aroma spoils everything else otherwise. We like eating these with pea, lentil and bean soup.

Sandwich spread made of carrots and beetroot

Some years we have had very large quantities of carrots and beetroots, and this gave me the idea of trying to make syrup from them. The vegetables are boiled down on a low heat. Now and again one spoons off floating vegetable pulp. Once the liquid has completely evaporated off you get a sandwich spread of very high quality. The aroma no longer smells anything like root vegetables though.

Freezing – quick and simple

I am particularly fond of freezing things because it is so quick – a great help when I have so many other things to do.

Strawberries, currants, raspberries and blackberries are packed in bags. I don't usually pack them away separately as I'm not going to use them separately.

Freezing is the simplest and quickest storage method

We use them to mix with yoghurt or quark (curd cheese) in winter. If you need fruit for decoration or baking cakes, freeze them separately first and only then pack them away together in bags. Then you can take them out singly. Peas and beans are vegetables suitable for freezing.

Dried fruit for cold winter evenings

Pears, apples, cherries and damsons dry very well and are particularly tasty in winter – as a snack or as fruit for baking.

Dried fruit is easy
to make yourself

Pears are quartered, keeping the peel on but removing the core. We peel apples and cut them into slices. Both apples and pears are dried in the oven at a low heat between 50° and 70°C.

We put cherries, together with their stones, in the side chamber of a wood-burning oven, where they dry within three or four days. In the case of damsons it is important to dry them with the stalk pointing upwards. If you don't do this the juice runs out and everything gets very sticky.

My favourite on bread: damson spread

I am especially fond of damson spread. First place a little sugar beet molasses in a pot, For five pounds of fresh, ripe plums you will need a 1-pound jar of sugar beet molasses. Then the de-stoned fruit are put in and everything is brought gently to the boil. Now it takes days, on a very low heat, for the fruit pulp to gradually simmer down into a con-centrate. This gives a valuable food suitable, in small quantities, for spreading on bread. This stimulates the metabolism and, primarily, the digestion.

Thun-ish cucumbers

We are always pleased if we harvest more cucumbers than we can eat, as pickled cucumbers are delicious in winter.

The cucumbers are washed and cut into slices. Then we put them in preserving jars with the desired herbs and spices, and fill up the jars with water. Our special spices are small twigs and leaves of oak and morello cherry, and vine leaves. We also add a dill umbel and a finely sliced onion to every jar – and of course salt and a shot of wine vinegar. The jars and contents have to be sterilized for an hour at 80°C. (The contents are cooked and as the bottle cools it is vacuum sealed.)

Mustard-seed cucumber

For one kilo of peeled cucumber we use a teaspoon of salt, a level teaspoon of mustard seeds and pieces of horse-radish root. First the cucumber, fully ripe, must be well peeled, and then one removes the seeds. If you use cucumbers that do not form seeds there is no need, of course, to remove them. Now slice the cucumbers into finger-thick strips and salt them. After 24 hours fill jars with the cucumber strips, but do not include the liquid that has formed.

Then add the mustard seeds and pieces of horseradish root, and fill with vinegar water (one tablespoon vinegar per litre of water). The cucumber jars should be sterilized for 40 minutes at 80°C. We like eating mustard-seed cucumber on bread at lunch or supper.

Bottling and freezing

As mentioned already, we freeze a great deal. Once the freezer is full we also bottle any remaining excess of vegetables, such as: cauliflower, beans, broccoli, peas, kohlrabi, carrots and celeriac – and of course cucumbers as described above.

Preserving vegetables by lactic acid fermentation

Many vegetables can be preserved by lactic acid fermentation, chiefly cabbage (sauerkraut) but also beans, kohlrabi, Savoy cabbage, carrots and beetroot. A large-scale trial recently showed that cucumbers preserved like this keep very well and taste very good if both the harvest and also the cutting and preserving is done on blossom and fruit days. The preserved cucumbers harvested and preserved on root days had a bitter smell, while those from leaf days dissolved in the lactic acid fluid. That is why we carry out all the work described only on blossom and fruit days, including the cutting of cabbage for sauerkraut.

Here is where it all started: my first garden in Marburg in 1949

Making sauerkraut yourself

The beds and fields for our cabbage are given 1000 kg of completely rotted cow manure compost per hectare (100 kg per 100 sq. m). During the growing period the plants are given the biodynamic spraying preparations (horn manure and horn silica) and we also spray them with teas made of yarrow, camomile, stinging nettle and dandelion blossom (see pages 26–7). Sowing, transplanting and all cultivation work is done on leaf days, but the cabbage is harvested on blossom or fruit days. The same applies to the shredding and preserving process.

How to make it: First shred the cabbage. The amount one can hold in two hands is placed in a clay pot. Now add 20 juniper berries, a pinch of cumin seed, 10 slices of apple, a few pieces of diced carrot and a level teaspoon of salt.

Next crush the cabbage with a wooden potato masher until the juice is expelled.

Again put as much cabbage into the pot as can be held in two hands, add the same ingredients again and mash as

On blossom or fruit days we place sauerkraut in preserving pots

Our 'Fire' from a home-made Thun-ish recipe is delicious for those who like things hot and spicy

`Thun-ish Fire'
Better than ketchup

Fruit and vegetables store well in a cool cellar

before. Continue like this until the pot is full or you have used all the cabbage. Mashing of the first layer takes longest, and the fluid is expelled quicker from every further layer.

Now fill the pot to the top with water, and place the lid on it.

It is best to place the pot in a warm place, at a temperature of 18°–20°C. When it starts bubbling you know that the chemical changes are occurring.

After two weeks the cabbage is usually ready. Don't forget to check the pot and add more water as necessary.

Sauerkraut contains a good deal of vitamin C. Raw sauerkraut broth acts as a laxative.

Thun-ish Fire

We like making our ketchup ourselves. We have a type for every taste and, because we often have visitors from Hungary and Slovenia, we make one especially for 'fiery' guests – our 'Thun-ish Fire'.

Tomatoes, paprika, apples, peppers, onions and aubergines are mixed together – and for people who like it hot we add a lot of chilli peppers!

How to make it: All fruits and vegetables are put through the mincer together with a little garlic. Add some salt and sugar, fill glass jars or bottles with the mixture and sterilize for two hours at 90°C.

WINTER

TIPS FOR SPECIFIC PLANTS

Greenhouse care

In the greenhouse we have to take particular care of the soil, as it is used heavily and we cannot adhere to crop rotation in the way necessary to maintain its health.

In the late autumn we spread one bucket of compost to 2 sq. m. It must be well rotted to aid the soil structure and is worked into the topsoil.

The best celeriac of all

When the sun is in Goat (from 18 January to 13 February) this would be

You get fat celeriac if you sow it with the sun in Goat (18 January to 13 February) and the moon in Bull, Virgin or Goat

the ideal time to sow celeriac on root days – and they would get nice and plump. Unfortunately you can only do this in a slightly heated greenhouse. We don't do it, as it's too expensive. But anyone who is heating a greenhouse anyway should try it.

When the sun is in Waterman (14 February to 10 March), plants tend to shoot. A cool June night is often enough to stop the 'bulbs' developing further.

Multi-talented garlic

Garlic is said to have an extraordinary number of positive properties – enough to make your head whirl. It prevents arteriosclerosis and other age-related problems, keeps you young, extends life expectancy, and so on and so forth. But unfortunately eating it leaves the after-effect of an unpleasant body odour, which many – including me – don't care for. I once ate a bowl of lentil soup well spiced with garlic. A couple of days later I wondered where the garlic smell was coming from. I sniffed here and there, but couldn't work out what was causing it – until I found it was my own skin. Since then I only eat a little garlic, even though I like its taste. Milk is said to counteract the smell, but I'm not sure whether it only combats it in the mouth or whether one would need to take a milk bath!

Sowing tomatoes

The best time to sow tomatoes is on fruit days when the sun is in Waterman –

Here I am in 1975, at the trial field in Gisselberg

from 14 February to 10 March. The fruit from these plants ripen best. If we choose days when the sun is in Fishes (11 March to 17 April), the plants will be more susceptible to fungal infection and slower to ripen.

Cuttings for grafting

If you want to take cuttings to graft onto fruit trees or vines, it is best to choose frost-free nights in the non-planting period. Fruit days are the best for this, but the blossom day influence is also suited to this work. Store the cuttings in a cool, damp place until you are ready to use them.

If you graft scions during the non-planting period, forces are focused in the upper parts of trees and bushes. If you also choose fruit days you will be rewarded by healthy growth and rich harvests.

Rose hips have remarkable healing forces

If we are going to use rose hips we harvest them on fruit days during the non-planting period. We make tea from the seeds which stimulates kidney function and water elimination. The red fruit pulp, together with apple juice and sugar, makes a delicious rose hip jam, which is very rich in vitamins.

Rose hips can be widely used, for instance as soup or jam. We make tea from the seeds

Sloe and milk mix

I am especially fond of sloes. This is a Saturn fruit and helps combat colds and chills, and also stimulates blood formation.

The fruits are a real treasure. However, they should only be harvested after a few frosty nights, for then they grow sweet. From sloes we make fruit syrup, juice and jelly. A sloe and milk mixture tastes very good, and is simple to make: shake together sloe juice with milk and a little honey – and there you are.

A portrait of the vine

We don't have much experience of vine cultivation in a small-scale garden but I believe that findings from commercial wine-growing could equally apply to the smaller garden.

Our wine-growers spray the cow-pat pit (barrel) mixture on the soil on root days when compost is being spread in the autumn (1000 kg per hectare).

In the spring the soil should, where possible, be cultivated on fruit days, accompanied at the same time by application of horn manure.

We recommend the planting period for harvesting grapes – and here the Lion days are best.

Subsequently, during the growing season, we treat the vine leaves with yarrow and dandelion blossom teas once each on flower days in the morning, and with camomile tea once in the morning

on a fruit day, and stinging nettle and oak bark tea once each in the morning on leaf days.

To promote the development of flower buds for the following year we spray the surrounding soil with valerian tea around the time of St John's, on a blossom day in the evening.

These treatments give healthy fruits of sound quality.

The effect of teas in vine and fruit cultivation

Yarrow blossom tea: We spray this tea on the leaves in the morning on a blossom day. This activates the potassium process and thus strengthens the plant. It also allows us to do without sulphur-based sprays.

Camomile blossom tea: Sprayed in the

Our field tests are labour-intensive. In this trial we tested the effect of different teas on the vine

morning on fruit days, this stimulates the calcium process, strengthening the plant and enabling us to do without copper-based sprays.

Stinging nettle tea: Spraying leaves with the tea in the morning on leaf days stimulates the plant's vital forces. This has a beneficial effect on the iron and manganese process.

Dandelion blossom tea: By spraying this on vine leaves in the morning on leaf days, we strengthen the silica process, leading to foliage with greater strength and resistance to disease. Parasites find it harder to penetrate the leaves, which can be a particular problem in wet years.

Valerian blossom tea: Around the time of St John's we water this into the soil

Our field tests are labour-intensive. In this trial we tested the effect of different teas on the vine

where vines, fruit trees and berry bushes are growing. This has a positive effect on flower bud formation. This tea also helps reduce damage from night frosts, and we spray it directly onto plants after a frost, triggering a warmth process. Since plants usually go limp after treatment, we have to water them well a few hours later.

Cutting Christmas trees at the right time

If one wishes to cut Christmas trees for one's own use, the best time to do so is on blossom days during the non-planting period – preferably shortly before Christmas. This helps the trees to stay beautiful for longer. If trees are being

harvested for commercial sale, you should at least try to choose days that do not fall within the planting period, when the sap is concentrated in the upper parts of the tree. This gives a better quality and allows them to survive longer. Often such trees even put forth shoots after being cut, and emanate a delicate scent of fir.

The nature of trees

In trees too you can rediscover a fourfold quality (see pages 4–7). This manifests in the earth sap (fluid in the earth which rises into the tree), the wood sap (fluid transported into the leaves), the life sap (in the leaves themselves), and the cambium as the fourth 'stream'.

The connection of each type of sap with the elements is as follows: earth sap = connection to earth; wood sap = connection to the watery element; life sap = connection to the element of light/air; cambium = connection to the warmth element.

We can also observe this fourfold quality in trunk slices: first comes the bark, then the cortex and bast, which enclose and protect the bearer of fertility, the cambium layer.

Compost application per se should occur via the bark, through the proven 'paste-coating' method (see page 78). Applied to tree roots, plants such as stinging nettle, English marigold (calendula), phacelia and nasturtium have a harmonizing effect and keep pests at bay.

The horn manure preparation ensures

The tree — a world in itself

that earth and wood sap find the right mutual relationship. Via warmth and light, silica supports the plant's connection with its surroundings, and helps zodiac forces to work in the cambium. When felling trees and grafting scions, we take account of cosmic influences (see pages 10–11). All these measures are very helpful for trees and give them the best possible conditions for good, healthy growth.

APPENDIX

Assigning plants to the four groups

Plant	Group		Plant	Group
Apple	Fruit plant		Beetroot	Root plant
Apricot	Fruit plant		Blackberries	Fruit plant
Artichoke (globe)	Blossom plant		Blueberry	Fruit plant
Oriental mustard	Leaf plant		Broad beans	Fruit plant
Asparagus	Leaf plant		Broccoli	Blossom plant
Aubergine	Fruit plant		Brussels sprouts	Leaf plant

Viola, blossom plant

Apple, fruit plant

Cress, leaf plant

Carrot, root plant

Camomile, blossom plant

Artichoke, blossom plant

Plant	Group	Plant	Group
Bush beans	Fruit plant	Cucumber	Fruit plant
Cabbage	Leaf plant	Currants	Fruit plant
Carrot	Root plant	Endive	Leaf plant
Cauliflower	Leaf plant	Fennel (herb)	Leaf plant
Celeriac	Root plant	Flower bulbs	Blossom plant
Celery	Leaf plant	Flowering perennials	Blossom plant
Chard	Leaf plant	Flowering shrubs (e.g. forsythia)	Blossom plant
Cherry	Fruit plant	French beans	Fruit plant
Chicory	Leaf plant	Garlic	Root plant
Chinese cabbage	Leaf plant	Gooseberries	Fruit plant
Chives	Leaf plant	Grains	Fruit plant
Cos lettuce	Leaf plant	Grass	Leaf plant
Courgette	Fruit plant	Greengage	Fruit plant
Cranberry	Fruit plant		

Cucumber, fruit plant

Morning glory, blossom plant

Red radish, root plant

English marigold, blossom plant

Beetroot, root plant

Aubergine, fruit plant

Plant	Group	Plant	Group
Hazelnut	Fruit plant	Lettuce	Leaf plant
Herbaceous perennials	Leaf plant	Marrow	Fruit plant
Herbs, flowering	Blossom plant	Melon	Fruit plant
Herbs, leaf	Leaf plant	Nectarine	Fruit plant
Horseradish	Root plant	New Zealand spinach	Leaf plant
Jerusalem artichoke	Root plant	Onion	Root plant
Jostaberry	Fruit plant	Orache	Leaf plant
Kale	Leaf plant	Pak choi	Leaf plant
Kiwi	Fruit plant	Parsnip	Root plant
Kohlrabi	Leaf plant	Peach	Fruit plant
Lamb's lettuce	Leaf plant	Pear	Fruit plant
Leek	Leaf plant	Peas	Fruit plant
Lentil	Fruit plant	Peppers	Fruit plant

Dicentra, blossom plant

Lemon balm, leaf plant

Onion

Lettuce, leaf plant

Primula, blossom plant

Aloe vera, leaf plant

Plant	Group	Plant	Group
Plums/damsons	Fruit plant	Soya beans	Fruit plant
Potato	Root plant	Spinach beet	Leaf plant
Pumpkin	Fruit plant	Spinach	Leaf plant
Quince	Fruit plant	Strawberry	Fruit plant
Radicchio	Leaf plant	Sunflower	Blossom plant
Radish	Root plant	Swede	Root plant
Raspberry	Fruit plant	Sweet chestnuts	Fruit plant
Rhubarb	Leaf plant	Sweetcorn	Fruit plant
Rocket	Leaf plant	Sweet potato	Root plant
Roses	Blossom plant	Tomato	Fruit plant
Runner beans	Fruit plant	Turnip	Root plant
Salsify	Root plant	Vine	Fruit plant
Shallot	Root plant	Walnut	Fruit plant

Cherry, fruit plant

Sage, leaf plant

Pears, fruit plant

Thuja, leaf plant

Tomato, fruit plant

Redcurrant, fruit plant

Addresses for ordering biodynamic preparations

Biodynamic Agricultural Association,
Painswick Inn Project, Gloucester Street,
  Stroud, Glos, GL5 1QG
Tel: ++44 (0)1453 759501
email: office@biodynamic.org.uk

Addresses in other countries

Australia
Biodynamic AgriCulture Australia, PO
  Box 54, Bellingen, N.S.W. Australia
  2454
Tel. ++61-266-55 05 66 Fax. -55 85 51
email: poss@midcoast.com.au

Brazil
Instituto Biodinamico, Rua Amando de
  Barros, 321 BR-18603-970, Botucatu
  SP Tel: ++55 14 822 5066
Fax: ++55 14 822 5066
email: ibd@laser.com.br

Canada
Society for Biodynamic Farming &
  Gardening in Ontario, R.R #4 Bright,
  Ontario NOJ 1BO
Tel/fax (519) 684-6846

Egypt
Egyptian Biodynamic Association,
  Heliopolis, El Horreya, PO Box 2834,
  Cairo, Egypt
Tel: + 20 2280 79 94
Fax: + 20 2280 69 59
email: ebda@sekim.com

France
Movement de Culture Biodynamique, 5,
  Place de la Gare, Colmar, F-68000,
  France
Tel: + 33 389 24 36 41
Fax: + 33 389 24 27 41
email: Biodynamis@wanadoo.fr

Germany
Forschungsring für Biologisch-
  Dynamische Wirtschaftsweise e. V.,
  Brandschneise 2
D-64295, Darmstadt
Tel: 49 6155 841241 Fax: 49 84 69 11

Holland
Vereniging voor Biologisch Dynamische
  Landbouw, Postbus 17,
  Diederichslaan 25
NL-3970 AA Driebergen
Tel. 0031-34 35-3 17 40
Fax. 0031 3435 16943
email: bd.vereniging@ecomarkt.nl
email: kraayhof@worldaccess.nl

India
Biodynamic Agriculture Association of
  India, 31 Signals Vihar, Mhow, MP
  453442, India
Tel: + 91 7324 746 64
Fax: + 91 7324 731 33

Ireland
Biodynamic Agricultural Association in
  Ireland, The Watergarden,
  Thomastown, Co. Kilkenny, Ireland

Tel: + 353 565 4214
Fax: + 353 508 73424

Italy
*Assoziazione per l'Agricultura
Biodinamica*, Via Vasto 4, I –20121,
Milano
Tel: + 39 02 2900 2544
Fax: + 39 02 2900 0692

New Zealand
*The Biodynamic Farming and
Gardening Association in NZ Inc,*

PO Box 39045, Wellington Mail
Centre, NZ
Tel: + 64 4 589 5366
Fax: + 64 4 589 5365
email: biodynamics@clear.net.nz

South Africa
*The Biodynamic Association of
Southern Africa*, PO Box 115,
Paulshof ZA-2056
Tel: + 27 118 0371 91
Fax: + 27 118 0371 91

Blossom plants love compost. We get beautiful flowers that blossom for a long time if we spread well-rotted compost in autumn, during the planting period – naturally on blossom days, when all other cultivation work should be also carried out for these plants (see page 75)

APPENDIX

Sweden
Biodynmiska Föreningen, Skillebyholm,
 S-15391, Järna, Sweden
Tel: + 46 8551 51225
Fax: + 46 8551 51227

Switzerland
*Landwirtschafliche Abteilung am
 Goetheanum*, Hügelweg 59, CH-4143,
 Dornach
Tel: + 41 61 706 4212
Fax: + 41 61 7061 42 15
email: landw.abteilung@goetheanum.ch

USA
*Biodynamic Farming and Gardening
 Association Inc*, Building 1002B,
 Thoreau Center, The Presido, PO Box
 29135, San Francisco, CA 94129 –
 0135
Tel: + 880 561 7797
Fax: + 880 561 7796
email: biodynamics@aol.com
www.biodynamics.com

Josephine Porter Institute
PO Box 133
Woolwine
VA 24185-0133

Addresses for ordering the sowing and planting calendar

*The Biodynamic Sowing and Planting
 Calendar* by Maria Thun is published
 in the UK by Floris Books, 15 Harrison
 Gardens, Edinburgh EH11 1SH
Tel: 0131 337 2372
Fax: 0131 347 9919
email: floris@florisbooks.co.uk

USA
SteinerBooks, PO Box 960, Herndon,
 VA 20172-0960
Tel: 800 856 8664
Fax: 703 661 1501
email: service@steinerbooks.org

INDEX

Page references in **bold** refer to illustrations

SPRING

SUMMER

AUTUMN

WINTER